crafting
wreaths
at home

COUNTRY LIVING

crafting wreaths at home

Text by Arlene Hamilton Stewart
Photography by Keith Scott Morton
Styling by Christine Churchill

HEARST BOOKS

A Division of Sterling Publishing Co., Inc.

NEW YORK

This book was previously published as a hardcover under the title
Country Living Handmade Wreaths: Decorating Throughout the Year

Produced by Smallwood & Stewart, Inc., New York City
Editor: Carrie Chase
Art Director: Tomek Lamprecht
Designer: Gretchen Mergenthaler

Special thanks to the Webb House, Orient Point, New York

Library of Congress Cataloging-in-Publication Data
Available upon request.

10 9 8 7 6 5 4 3 2 1

First paperback edition 2003
Published by Hearst Books
A Division of Sterling Publishing Company, Inc.
387 Park Avenue South, New York, N.Y. 10016

Country Living and Hearst Books are trademarks owned by
Hearst Magazines Property, Inc., in USA, and Hearst Communications, Inc.,
in Canada.

www.countryliving.com

Distributed in Canada by Sterling Publishing
c/o Canadian Manda Group, One Atlantic Avenue, Suite 105
Toronto, Ontario, Canada M6K 3E7
Distributed in Australia by Capricorn Link (Australia) Pty. Ltd.
P.O. Box 704, Windsor, NSW 2756 Australia

Text set in Galliard

Printed in Singapore

ISBN 1-58816-289-3

table of contents

foreword

It warms my heart to drive by a house in the middle of summer and see a wreath hanging from the front door. Of course I love seeing wreaths in winter, too, but I think it is wonderful that more and more people have started to display wreaths year-round.

Hanging a wreath on a front door is one of the easiest ways to say, "Come in, sit down, and relax." Of course, there's really no reason for a wreath to appear only on a door. Just as they are right in every season, they are right for every room. Wreaths can be dramatically simple, sized to fit into a little nook, or lushly abundant, to become the center of attention in a room.

There's really no reason to buy a wreath because wreaths are so easy (and fun) to make. Unlike sewing or baking, there are few formal, hard-and-fast instructions to wreath-making. You can make a wreath by hand simply by twisting a piece of grapevine into a circle, but wreaths are also a great way to make creative use of favorite flowers, botanicals, buttons. There's a whole world of materials just waiting to be transformed into a wreath with the aid of a glue gun or a few pieces of floral wire. In fact, I think collecting the materials—scouting around farmer's markets and backyards, or rummaging through remnants from other craft projects—may be just as much fun as making the wreaths themselves.

I do hope you'll be inspired to bring wreaths into your life and living spaces.

Rachel Newman

Editor Emerita, *Country Living*

introduction

No longer limited to the front door at Christmas, wreaths can flourish throughout the house, throughout the year. For every season there is a wreath: holly in winter, pussy willow in spring, lavender in summer, and Indian corn in autumn. For every room there is a wreath: gingerbread boys in a holiday kitchen, soothing herbs for bedrooms. For every occasion there is a wreath: bridal wreaths, birthday wreaths, remembrance wreaths, Mother's Day, Valentine's Day, and Christmas wreaths. Wreaths convey sentiment, say thank you, cheer up a loved one, welcome guests. And, whether they be immense or diminutive, a circle, oval, diamond, or square, wreaths have one thing in common—they're all handmade.

It's this quality that gives wreaths so much charm. When my daughter and I started to make wreaths at home, even our earliest efforts delighted us. It's really hard not to love a wreath. One of the few remaining hold-outs against mass-production, wreaths reflect the personality of the individual wreath-maker and should never look "professional." And there are so many different styles of wreaths—they can be elaborate heirloom projects requiring time and patience, or loose and free, whipped up in a moment of pure inspiration.

If anything can be said to be a time-honored tradition, it's wreath-making. Well over two thousand years ago, people were weaving wreaths of leaves and grains to celebrate important occasions and religious holidays. So timeless are many of these early wreaths that they resemble designs still popular today—with a few distinct differences. Long ago, wreaths were displayed on the head, not in the home. They had great symbolic significance. The circular shape of wreaths represented eternity, regeneration, and purity—

as well as victory and glory. Even the materials from which wreaths were made were symbolic. Since most ancient cultures revered trees as a source of divine energy, the earliest wreaths were fashioned from boughs, leaves, and sprigs. Victorious athletes from the Greek Olympics sported crowns of leaves from trees in the host cities. Laurel singled out the proud winners of competitions in the arts, music, and poetry.

As a bridal tradition, the head wreath has few peers. Viewed as a symbol of innocence because of its unbroken circular shape, the wreath was a necessity for nearly every ancient bride. Greeks of long ago were besotted by roses; in their culture, red roses symbolized love and desire, white represented purity. Smart brides took their vows wearing wreaths of both colors. In ancient Rome, halos of grain, an enduring symbol of fertility, were donned by groom and bride alike. The bridal wreath tradition lived on—in the fifth century, English bridesmaids wove aromatic wreaths of garlic, chives, rosemary, and dill mingled with roses and marigolds. Much later, in 1840, a rapturous Queen Victoria married wearing a halo of orange blossoms and diamonds entwined in her hair.

It's not entirely clear when the wreath as headdress also became the symbol of welcome for the home. One thought is that the wreath as wall decoration was an outgrowth of the ancient Germanic tradition of celebrating the winter holidays by adorning homes with boughs of evergreens: fir, balsam, holly, and pine. Because evergreens never lose their leaves, they came to symbolize eternity, and it was deemed lucky to imbue the home with a bit of green during the winter solstice. At some point, it was only natural that a resourceful homeowner would see the value in decorating the inside and outside of his home with a combination of both powerful symbols—the evergreen and the circle—united in a wreath. Since then, wreaths have only become more popular.

The projects in this book are intended to entertain you and excite your interest in wreath-making. View them as starting points; like most creative people, you'll probably find yourself altering the ideas as you go along—and that's a good thing. Wreaths don't have to be slavish replicas in order to be successful. Favorite color combinations, fabrics, flowers, and materials are part of the personality a wreath-maker brings to a project.

An inspiring range of materials is available to the wreath-maker. Going far beyond the stock evergreen wreath with a red bow, the winter holiday wreath can be fashioned from hundreds of jingle bells or a trayful of gingerbread boys. A collection of mother-of-pearl buttons comes out of the button box and onto a satin-covered oval wreath. Mother Nature never fails to supply us with magnificent materials: memories of seaside vacations wash back with a seashell wreath; a simple bittersweet wreath warms us with the colors of autumn.

Making a wreath is not difficult, and after reviewing the material in Wreath-making Techniques you should be able to hop right into a project without worrying about mistakes. If anything untoward does occur, remember that often wreaths can be taken apart and remade, or the materials recycled. Mistakes also add to the charm of the wreath. One note of warning: wreath-making can become an addiction. Fortunately, life offers an abundance of happy occasions—and they each deserve a wreath.

— *Arlene Hamilton Stewart*

chapter one

making wreaths

As long as there have been celebrations, there have been wreaths. Sitting under a shady tree on a summer's afternoon, a young miss in Shakespeare's day would wind halos of daisies (then known as day's ease) into garlands for friends' birthdays. Victorian brides, fluent in the "language" of flowers, decked pews with wreaths of rosemary hoping to ensure marital fidelity.

Until the advent of hot glue guns and Styrofoam bases, wreaths were made entirely by hand, with straw, twigs, flowers, and other natural materials twisted into circles, then fastened with strings, vines, and rope. Even though wreath-making is an ancient tradition, fortunately for the present-day wreath-maker several modern conveniences exist.

This chapter addresses the technical aspects of wreath-making. It's not a complicated process; in fact, there are only three basic elements—the base, the material, and the means of attachment. Included here is advice on how to assemble wreaths, how to hang them, and how to care for them. In addition, this chapter has tips on drying, preserving, and pressing flowers and herbs so that you can build up an inventory of materials.

bases

Bases are the backbone of every wreath, and it's important to fit the base to the project. This means considering the kinds of materials you will be working with and the final look you would like. Some wreaths technically have no base at all—because the wreath itself is also the base. Think of grapevine wreaths and bittersweet wreaths, where lengths of vines are twisted around and around to make simple wreaths. But most wreaths require a base, and every base has different qualities.

Bases are either ready-made and purchased at craft stores, or constructed at home with some type of frame or found object pressed into service. Ready-made bases do save time and are very strong, especially wire box frames; certainly, using a ready-made base does not diminish the quality of the project. When craft stores have sales, stock up. Practically every base you could make is available ready-made—plus some you can't really make yourself.

Some projects call for a custom base, which are fun to make, especially if you're a purist who loves doing everything from scratch. Making bases is not difficult, and once you start creating your own wreaths, you'll probably discover new ways to make bases.

Extruded foam, also known as Styrofoam, bases come in many diameters, shapes, sizes, and with varying densities. Some of the circular Styrofoam bases are sold cut in half lengthwise, giving you two circles, each with a flat side, which is helpful if you're making a flat wreath. Otherwise, you need to join them together, usually by tightly wrapping floral wire around them. Styrofoam is not suitable for all projects; hot glue from a gun can melt it, and Styrofoam can break up when picks are inserted into it. Use it for lighter wreaths, such as dried flowers, or when you want to wrap the base with ribbon, as we did in the Cameo Gift Wreath (page 97).

One of the most common ready-made bases is the wire box frame. Despite the box in its name, this is a circular base. It's made from two or more circles of wire connected with metal spacers. The frames come in different sizes; the larger ones are especially good for making bigger, thicker, more impressive wreaths because of their strength. The bottoms of some wire box frames have a gentle scoop, which makes them ideal for cradling large materials such as

The most commonly used bases for wreaths, clockwise from the top: Styrofoam bases, in two of their many shapes; a wire box frame; a grapevine base; and straw bases in two sizes. Floral picks rest inside the Styrofoam base.

gourds, pinecones, apples, shells, etc. Often, this base is decorated with a covering of dried Spanish moss, evergreens, craft straw, baby's breath, or statice to hide the metal before other materials are added (although the Gingerbread Boy Wreath on page 92 features a metal base sprayed with gold paint and used as a "baker's rack").

You've probably seen wire wreath bases with clamps and thought they were too scary-looking to bring home. But these bases are sought after by wreath-makers for their versatility. They're especially good for large wreaths where you want a consistent look rather than a random one. Their sturdy clamps grip the stems of plant materials, and they also hold blocks of Styrofoam into which you can insert dried materials—particularly handy for making wreaths for a table centerpiece.

Another type of wire base is the simple wire ring base, which consists of a single piece of wire curved into a circle. This wire frame is appropriate for delicate wreaths of fresh flowers such as lilies-of-the-valley and roses, or for covering with dried Spanish moss as a base for other wreaths. Some stores carry wire ring bases, but they are easy to make out of heavy #16-gauge wire purchased from a hardware store, or from an ordinary wire coat hanger. You need a length of wire that equals the circumference of your wreath plus about

4 inches. Shape the wire into the size you want, leaving 2 inches at each end. With a pair of pliers, bend back the extra 2 inches on each end to make two loops. Hook the loops together and twist the ends around the ring.

Ready-made straw bases are the workhorses of the wreath world, offering the craftsperson lots of options. Inexpensive, densely packed, rounded, full, and very sturdy, they are available in a variety of sizes. When making wreaths that involve inserting a lot of material, either with floral picks or pins, straw wreaths are ideal; they firmly hold the material in place. Since making a straw base from scratch is messy work, choose ready-mades when possible. However, kids seem to love making them, and sometimes you need a custom-made straw base, as with the Indian Corn Wreath (page 78). This large and heavy required a strong base that was also somewhat flat. A wire box frame underneath the straw provided extra strength.

You can make straw bases with frames or without. Whenever you work with straw, first cover a flat surface with newspaper. A base made purely of straw requires long pieces of straw and green floral wire. Take a generous handful of straw and wrap the wire once around the straw. Knot the wire to keep it from unraveling. Continue taking new handfuls of straw, overlapping them as you wrap them with wire. Be sure to pull the wire tightly. As you work, curve the straw into a ring shape. Where both ends meet, carefully join with overlapping straw.

To make a straw base on a wire box frame, purchase a frame in the size you want, along with a package of craft straw. These are both standard items in craft stores. With a paddle of green floral wire, tie one end to the wire frame. Add handfuls of straw onto the base while firmly wrapping the wire around it. Make the handfuls consistent and wind the wire at 1- to 2-inch intervals. At the end, twist the wire to close.

When you want a look that's natural and informal, vine bases are the answer. In fact, many are so beautiful, they need no embellishment at all. Available in many sizes and shapes, vine bases can be made from thick, beefy vines or from smaller, more delicate branches. Look for those that have a balance to them, with tendrils that are not jagged or broken off.

To make these bases at home, you need a supply of vines. While you can use nearly any vine to make a wreath, avoid those that are unknown to you. (Since I discovered that I'm allergic to Virginia creeper, this vine does not appear in my repertoire.) Staying with familiar vines—grape, wisteria, honeysuckle, or bittersweet—is recommended.

All vines must be pliable in order to work with them. If they aren't fresh or feel brittle, soak them in water until they are supple (between 12 to 24 hours). I do this in a big tub in my backyard; lacking that you could use a sink. Strip off any leaves before soaking, being careful to leave the tendrils intact. Remove the vines from the water and dry them a little before you start your wreath.

There are different techniques for making vine bases. As you become more experienced with vines, you'll discover the technique that works for you. One is wrapping the base. In this basic method, you select a long sturdy vine and make a circle in the size you want. Continue by wrapping the vine around the base circle. When you are finished, tuck the end in. Then, pick up another length and continue wrapping—in the same direction— adding more vines until you have the volume base you want. Whether you wrap the vines close or spaced apart is a design decision that's up to you. You can vary this base by forming the circle with a number of vines. Take three or four vines at once and shape them into a circle, then continue wrapping these around. Tuck in the ends, then pick up additional vines and keep wrapping.

The tied base is another vine base option. Take strands of vines and tie them together (instead of wrapping). Make a circle with the tied vines in the size you want, then, holding the circle together with one hand, make another circle of the vines over the first until you reach the volume base you want. If you want more volume, add new vines after securing the base. Some wreath-makers like to secure their vine bases by wrapping even vines around them. Others like green floral wire. To do that, wrap a spool of wire in several places around the base, then conceal the wire with a long strand of vine.

When you want to make a wreath with living plants or flowers, a time-tested way to do this is with a moss-filled ring, which provides moisture for the plants. To make a base with a 16-inch diameter, you need a rectangle of chicken wire that is 10 inches by 54 inches, and about a quart of fresh sphagnum moss. Soak the moss for 15 to 20 minutes, then wring out excess water. Lay the chicken wire down and place the moss in a strip down the middle of the wire. Carefully fold the wire over the moss to make a tube, twisting the ends of the wire together. Shape the tube into a circle, connecting the end wires. After you add the plant material, water well.

For a fresh-flower wreath, the chicken wire could be filled with floral oasis (florists' clay) in place of the moss. This dark green substance absorbs water, allowing flower stems to receive extra moisture. Available from craft stores or florists, floral oasis comes in various sizes and shapes. It must be saturated in advance of constructing the wreath. Also, because it becomes heavy and damp, it's not suitable for every project.

The Seashell Wreath (page 56) required a flat wooden base for two reasons: the wood was rigid and would support the weight of the shells, plus the flat shape would hang well against a wall, allowing the wreath to have that same lovely feeling as a shoreline with shells washing upon it. Craft stores carry some wooden bases, but they come in limited sizes. If you plan to make a project that requires a wooden base, have one made. This may sound more daunting than it is: many craft stores have suppliers who make things for them. The base for the Seashell Wreath is not difficult to create. It was cut from 3/8-inch plywood, but you could also use 1/2-inch.

Sometimes a wreath base is constructed of a material that's really something else, as with the Button Wreath (page 47). It has an embroidery hoop as its base, which was perfect for the Victorian nature of the covering materials.

Be creative in what you consider a base— as long as it is strong enough to hold your materials, almost anything can become a base for a beautiful wreath.

tools & attachments

Fortunately, wreath-making is not a craft that requires a vast inventory of tools, an elaborate workshop, expensive start-up costs, or even lessons. But, as you fall more and more under the spell of wreath-making, you will find tools that make your work easier, and you'll find yourself reaching for them over and over again. Most of these tools are used to attach materials to bases because that's the technical essence of wreath-making. Indeed, the wreath-maker's biggest quandary often is: how will I attach this? Securing materials to bases is critical. No one wants to spend hours making a beautiful wreath, only to have it fall apart in a matter of minutes.

One of the first issues to resolve before making a wreath is to match the weight of the materials to the strength of the base; heavier materials need firmer support than lighter ones. Keeping that in mind, the following tools will be invaluable in attaching and supporting materials to bases.

If I were to name the single most useful tool for the wreath-maker, it would have to be the hot glue gun. This small electrical tool, available in hardware stores and craft stores, allows you to quickly and permanently secure materials to a base—even cumbersome materials such as gourds. Because its glue dries so quickly, the glue gun lets you position materials as no other glue would—you can stand shells on end such as in the Seashell Wreath (page 56), make patterns with bulky items like pinecones and ears of dried corn, or attach delicate rosebuds any way you want. Cumbersome or heavy objects can be attached in seconds; materials can be given interesting poses that make wreaths come alive, rather

Green floral tape, in the photograph at right, covers plant stems and camouflages unsightly wire bases. A paddle of #22-gauge green floral wire, at left, is used to attach materials to bases and create hangers. A wreath-maker can never keep enough of these two tools on hand.

than looking static; and nearly everyone can wield a glue gun, young or old. One press of its trigger and a dab of super strong, super fast-drying glue is released. All you have to master is how much glue to use to avoid drips, and how long to hold the materials in place.

When I made the Seashell Wreath, I wanted to use a profusion of shells. While ordinary white glue does a decent job of attaching lightweight materials, it takes a long time to dry. I knew the hot glue gun would hold the shells securely, allow me to position them upright, and the glue would dry quickly. I selected a speciality base of ³/₈-inch plywood, which was strong but would not overpower the shells by being too thick.

Glue guns are made with hot or low temperature settings. I've had great success with the low-temperature version—and judging from the occasional burn, it's hard to imagine how scalding the higher temperature glue gun gets. On the plus side, the hot-temperature glue guns allegedly make a more permanent bond than the low ones. I've never had a problem with the low setting, but the glue eventually will peel off glass, and it doesn't work well with metal. When buying a glue gun, which is reasonably priced, get one with a self-advancing glue stick; since glue guns use more glue than you would think, you want to keep a steady flow going. It's also helpful to purchase a large supply of glue sticks (preferably the long ones, so that you don't have to refill the gun as often).

Most glue guns are very simple to operate—just plug it in, heat it up, and go—but it's always best to carefully read the manufacturer's instructions before operating. When working with a glue gun, cover your work surface with newspaper to catch drips, and always leave the glue gun standing upright, like an iron. As with any electrical tool, be particularly careful using them around children.

Also high up on the list of wreath-making essentials is green floral wire. Part of so many wreaths and projects, this thin wire secures materials to bases, binds little bunches of botanicals together into sprigs, wraps picks

glue gun safety

Glue guns do get hot, so it is important to be very careful when using them. If hot glue gets on your skin, submerge the area in water, peel off the glue, and treat as you would any other burn: hold the affected area under cold running water or apply a cold compress, and if possible keep the burned area elevated above your heart. When making a wreath with a glue gun, consider keeping a bowl of water next to your work space, so that if you scald yourself you can quickly cool off.

to stems, attaches hangers, makes hangers—it never stops working! Since floral wire is such a necessity, purchase it in quantity. It comes on paddles or spools (usually 25 feet) at craft stores. It is available in different widths, termed gauges. The higher the gauge, the thinner the wire. Nearly all the wreaths in this book are made with #22-gauge wire, but #24 is also useful.

Pre-cut floral wire is perfect for attaching heavier objects, such as the pomegranates to the Ivy and Pomegranate Wreath (page 88), or for making artificial stems for delicate flowers. The pieces are usually 18 inches long and come in different gauges. I prefer the thicker #16- to #18-gauge wires for their strength. To make an artificial stem, cut a 12-inch piece of the floral wire and bend it into a U shape. Leaving at least 1 inch of the floral stem intact, take the wire, and with the U placed right below the flower head, wrap the other side of the wire, in closely spaced coils, around both the floral stem and the wire stem. Wrap the new stem in floral tape (see description below).

To cut your wires, you're going to need a pair of wire cutters. Most ordinary household scissors will cut through wire, but over time this ruins scissors. Look for a pair that fits into your hand and is easy to use. You may need a pair of clippers or pruning shears to cut through thick or woody stems on vines and other botanicals. Once you get involved with wreath-making, you'll always be sure to have in your backpack a pair of these or a Swiss army knife to clip any exciting discoveries made while walking through the woods or countryside.

Floral tape conceals wires and stems. It comes on rolls in brown, green, or white and is usually ½ inch wide. This thin, stretchy tape also lends extra support to flowers and botanicals. The wire base of the Bridal Wreath (page 62) is wrapped with floral tape.

When wreath-makers want to strengthen or lengthen stems, or reinforce clusters of materials, they reach for wooden floral picks. These are short pieces of green-colored wood with a length of wire attached to one end and a point at the other. They are invaluable for reinforcing delicate botanicals, such as the dried hydrangea clusters for the Blue Hydrangea Wreath (page 59). Lay the pick, point side down, aside the stem, then coil the wire all the way down the length of the pick. Carefully insert the pick into bases of straw, vines, or Styrofoam. U-shaped floral pins, which look a little like over-sized paper clips, can also be used to hold material to a base. They're good for pinning on ribbons, masses of moss, or any material you want to look loose.

A few more words about attaching material: While a glue gun was used to assemble many of the wreaths in this book, others were assembled by wiring with floral wire, a traditional manner of attachment, or by sewing, as with the Jingle Bell Wreath (page 101), a more non-traditional method.

When considering the means of attachment, think about the kinds of materials you are attaching in addition to their weight. For example, in the Porch Wreath (page 61), baskets that would be filled with living flowers were wired to the base with #22-gauge green floral wire. If they had been glued to the base, not as much air and circulation would get through to the plants.

The base you choose is often determined by how you plan to assemble the materials. With three dozen ears of miniature corn to be wired to the Indian Corn Wreath (page 78), the base had to be somewhat flat, strong, and, in keeping with the design,

rustic. A wire box frame, wired with straw, met all the requirements.

If you are attaching foundation material to a wire box frame, take a paddle of floral wire (#22-gauge is fine), tie the end of the wire to the frame, and wrap it around the material and the frame in coils 1 to 2 inches apart.

Cover a wire ring base before any materials are attached. Sometimes—if you're adding flowers—it's just a matter of wrapping the base with green floral tape. If you're making a moss base, take a handful of the moss, cover the metal, and wrap the wire around several times. Continue adding moss on the frame and wrapping until complete. To attach floral material, wrap the end of the floral wire to the base, then place a small cluster of material next to the base and continue wrapping. Add more clusters facing the same direction until the base is covered (attach the last cluster by gently lifting up the first). Cut the wire and weave the end into the back of the wreath.

materials

The concept of wreath-making has expanded so greatly that nearly everything becomes material for the wreath-maker: leaves of all kinds, fruits, berries, grasses, twigs, scented herbs, pods, seeds, and vegetables. There are gardens of flowers fresh, preserved, and pressed waiting to be made into wreaths. There are fabric wreaths, button wreaths, culinary wreaths, shell wreaths. There are wreaths of materials meant for just one very special day—like the Bridal Wreath (page 62) made of fresh roses—or wreaths of ever-lasting beauty, such as the Cameo Gift Wreath (page 97), meant to delight year after year.

Many wreath-makers have a special love for dried materials because of their lasting quality: pinecones, pods, dried stalks of wheat, dried herbs, strawflowers, Chinese lanterns, statice, love-in-a-mist, globe amaranth, and more. A tremendous amount of dried plant material is available commercially, or you can dry your own with selections from your gardens and rambles in fields, woods, and roadsides. Look for milkweed, goldenrod, thistle, multiflora rose hips, Queen Anne's lace, and more. Methods of drying and preserving are discussed in the section Drying Flowers (page 33).

To savor the glory of an herbal garden year round, is anything lovelier than an aromatic herbal wreath? A wonderful bonus for the wreath-maker, herbs both dried and fresh scent the air delightfully, and many can be used for culinary purposes, such as a version of the classic bay leaf wreath (page 84). Any cook worth her salt would love a wreath of dried thyme, basil, oregano, or sage (page 69). And certainly the traditional chili-pepper wreath is hard to live without. For centuries herbs have been used to soothe many ailments, and the fascination with aromatherapy makes herbal wreaths even more popular. You'll see how magnificent stems of lavender look—and smell—when swirled en masse in a Lavender Wreath (page 48).

Fruits and vegetables have certainly earned their places in the wreath world. Pomegranates, used in the Ivy and Pomegranate Wreath (page 88), age beautifully as you celebrate the winter holidays. Combine them with kumquats, oranges, and limes for a look that's straight out of Colonial Williamsburg. In fact, each Christmas many homes and shops of Colonial Williamsburg hang up festive wreaths that recall the wreaths of holidays past. Many of these wreaths are decorated with fruit nesting atop American and English boxwood. One of their most beautiful is a wreath of apples and holly berries on boxwood. At the Governor's Palace, a wreath of pomegranates framed with magnolia leaves and holly berries bids welcome to holiday visitors. The Christmas theme continues with a Boxwood Wreath (page 106), elegant enough for a governor's parlor—and your own.

The seasons too are a lavish provider of materials for wreaths. In the summer, the countryside comes to life with wildflowers and grasses—just avoid protected species. Autumn brings with it sharp nights and colors. Who could not fall under the spell of velvety dried cockscomb in all its shadings? One of the most beautiful wreaths I've ever seen was made entirely of cockscomb in a deep claret shade, and it went beyond regal just the way it was, with no ribbon or adornment. For centuries, autumn has been the time to honor the harvest by displaying some of its bounty. Simple swirls of wheat look wonderful, such as the Country Wheat Wreath (page 80), as would a wreath of oats or barley. Wreaths of colorful Indian corn come into play now. A trip to a local farm or garden center will provide a bounty of rich hues and textures.

Evergreens, the staple of the Christmas wreath, are readily available in garden centers. Among the easiest to find are hemlock, balsam, cedar, arbor vitae, hemlock, holly, Scotch pine, and white pine. You can also cut greens from your own property, or from that of generous friends. The Double-Sided Fir Wreath (page 95) was made from cuttings taken from an artistic neighbor's property in Katonah, New York. Most greens will last a long time on a wreath; indeed, in our town it's become the custom to leave Christmas wreaths up all winter, thus extending their tenure in office. If you would like to keep your wreath up outdoors for a while, try to make any bows of more weatherproof materials, rather than delicate silks and satins, which weather better inside, and remove any overtly holiday ornamentation.

christmas wreaths

The traditional evergreen wreath is beautiful on its own, which is why it is so ubiquitous at Christmastime on our front doors. However, it is easy to embellish a store-bought wreath with personal touches. Add a collection of ornaments or cookie cutters by tying them onto the fir branches or hanging them with little wire ornament hooks. Adding a few sprigs of dried flowers is an easy way to add color. Consider some small potatoes that have been burnished with gold leaf. For the holiday itself, insert some tropical Peruvian lilies (in water picks) to the wreath.

Many wreath-makers love the look of curly Spanish moss as a foundation on their wreaths. This dried moss is available at craft supply stores. It fills out spaces nicely, giving volume to bases. Sphagnum moss, which sometimes gets saturated in water before using, works well as a filler with chicken-wire bases. Moss from the garden can be added to wreaths of fresh flowers or herbs; garden moss is tucked into the Porch Wreath (page 61).

In addition to natural materials, there many other options available for the wreath-maker. The wreath of mother-of-pearl buttons (page 47) was inspired by a sister's vast collection of buttons. Too beautiful not to share or display, they were sewn onto creamy satin ribbon for a lovely, old-fashioned feeling. Make a wreath like this with buttons from a special dress, such as a wedding gown, or a baby's christening gown. A crazy quilt wreath can be sewn from scraps of velvets, brocades, or other fabrics with nostalgic value. Embroider the names of grandchildren on it and you've made a Mother's Day gift that's far more personal and valuable than anything bought in a store. Look around your own home; perhaps you have beautiful ribbons that could be made into a wreath, or beads that

would look festive strung together for Christmas. A vacation wreath of souvenirs and photographs would be a sweet way to remember those happy times.

To adorn your wreath, ribbons are the most traditional decoration, although many wreaths are so beautiful, they need no decoration at all. Today, ribbon is available in many sizes, colors, and fabrics. Wired ribbon is a blessing for the wreath-maker; because it's so flexible, it makes every bow look elegant. You can get this ribbon, also known as French ribbon, in many fabrics: silk, satin, cotton, etc. The Blue Hydrangea Wreath (page 59) is hung with shimmery streamers in lavender organdy, and the Cameo Gift Wreath (page 97) is made of wired French ribbon. Paper ribbons nicely complement wreaths of natural materials, such as bittersweet and grapevine. I'm particularly fond of fabric sashes on wreaths. I love their opulence, and for a more formal wreath, such as the twin pines (page 98), I sewed my own sashes. To give any wreath a country feeling, you can't miss with plaid ribbons. At Christmas, a jaunty bow or a piece of plaid entwined around evergreens seems to capture the merriment of the season.

design & display

When making a wreath, there are many design issues to consider, most of which are personal ones: what kind of materials you will have, where you will hang the finished creation. But before you begin your wreath venture ask yourself a couple of general questions: Will the base be a part of the design? Will the materials determine where and how the wreath will be hung?

In many wreaths, the base is partially exposed and thus becomes an important design element. Most natural bases are inherently handsome: twig, Spanish moss, and grapevine, in particular. They look wonderful with simple, rustic materials: plaid ribbons, fruits, nuts, ivy, dried flowers, and berries.

Wire bases, on the other hand, will probably need to be covered—camouflaged—with foundation material or floral tape before you apply decoration.

Consider materials for their longevity or fragility. If your wreath is meant to last only a short time—a fresh-flower wreath, for instance—design it with its placement in mind, keeping it out of bright sunlight to maximize its vibrancy. Delicate wreaths, or heirloom wreaths that you would like to save for years to come, should not be hung in high-traffic areas.

Needless to say, both the type of hanger and its placement on the wreath should be worked out before making the wreath. There are only three rules for hangers: one, the heavier the wreath, the stronger the hanger; two, the most successful hangers are the simplest; and three, if the hanger will be visible, it must enhance the wreath.

Keep in mind that if you're making wire hangers for the backs of wreaths, position them so very little, if any, of the wire shows when the wreath is hung. If that's not possible, camouflage the wire with a piece of ribbon or twine.

Sometimes wreaths will not be hung at all. The Bridal Wreath (page 62) was constructed on a simple wire base. Since it was destined to be draped—over the back of a bride's chair or on a front door knocker—there was no need for a hanger. (If necessary, however, it could have rested upon a nail in the wall or door.) Scented wreaths are most appreciated where their fragrances can be savored. A wreath of lavender is delightful by the top of a bed or next to the bathtub.

In the case of any wreath that's made with a poisonous substance, such as bittersweet, don't place it where children are likely to be present.

The ultimate destination of a wreath may determine its color and scale. Again, take the case of the Bridal Wreath; if it were to be hung on a white front door, a wreath of white roses might be too passive. Another bridal shade, such as light blush pink or a rich cream, would work better. A wreath meant for a barn door would probably need to be made in a larger size than one intended for a nook in a dining room.

One of the easiest ways to ensure success for your wreath is to construct it at eye level or display height. This gives you the same vantage point of the finished wreath as the viewer. Obviously, this is not easily done in the case of a gigantic eucalyptus wreath destined to be suspended high above a fireplace. But whenever possible, try to hang the wreath up before finishing it to see whether it's consistent, neat, and appealing from every angle. When working on a flat surface, one is apt to make different design decisions than if the wreath were in an upright position. That's another reason why adding the hanger at the beginning of the project is so important.

drying flowers, herbs & fruits

From the earliest Johnnie-jump-up in April to bunches of mums in November, my house is filled with flowers and herbs in various staging of drying, preserving, and pressing. Although nothing can ever match the radiance of fresh flowers, there are so many lovely things in the garden and countryside, it's worth trying to preserve them. Fortunately, there are easy methods to do this at home, so there's rarely a need for the wreath-maker to purchase expensive dried flowers.

The basic principle in all botanical preservation is to remove as much moisture as possible while retaining the most color and form. There are several different ways to do this. Whatever method you select, before starting, harvest only the best-looking specimens. Avoid anything that is torn, blemished, discolored, diseased, or past its peak. Young flowers are best, picked on a dry morning before the sun scorches them. To make the most natural wreaths, gather flowers in all stages of the blooming cycle, from buds to almost completely open. (Many flowers continue to open their buds as they dry.)

Before setting out to the garden or countryside, select a drying method and have the supplies prepared. Also, buckets of tepid water should be ready to receive freshly cut stems. Gather many more flowers than you think you'll need; some won't make the cut, while others may not dry well or may break when handled.

Pressing flowers is an old tradition, but one that is mysteriously under-used today. I love the country feeling of a pressed wreath made of old-fashioned flowers, the kind that might be growing outside a kitchen door. Although you can try to press virtually any flower, I've had the most success with those that have flattish thin petals such as pansies, buttercups, Johnnie-jump-ups, violets, and bleeding hearts, all of which bloom about the same time in April and May. Later in the summer, I've pressed Queen Anne's lace, cosmos, morning glory, salvia, statice, and bee balm. I've taken apart roses and zinnias, pressed the petals, then later reconstructed them. Herbs and leaves are also candidates for pressing, especially elegant ferns.

Very little is required to press flowers: a roll of super-absorbent paper towels and some heavy books should do the trick. Use plain paper towels, which won't transfer any ink onto the drying material, and look for towels with the least texture, so the flowers don't pick up an impression. Gather the blossoms and leaves early in the day when they're dry. As soon as possible, spread and flatten each one face down on three or four layers of paper towels laid out on a flat surface. Now is the time to arrange the stems and tendrils into whatever look you want; when dry, they're brittle and could break off. Carefully place a top layer of three to four sheets of paper towels over the material and weigh them down. Place piles of four or five heavy books on top. After ten days, you can remove some pansies, ferns, bleeding hearts, violets, and violet leaves. Other materials take longer. Experiment to learn what works best for you.

Once dried, pressed materials are super light-weight and apt to fly away. I left my first batch next to an open window, only to watch them flutter around like lazy butterflies. Because they're so fragile, you may feel more comfortable handling them with tweezers. If you wish to glue them, the smallest dab of white glue will work, or try a spray adhesive.

As pressed flowers age, they fade, going through stages from a rosy color to a faint sepia. After time, you may wish to replace your indoor garden with fresh specimens.

The most popular method of drying flowers is also the easiest: air drying by hanging them upside down in bunches. This method works best with flowers that dry naturally on the stem: delphinium, larkspur, lavender, corn flowers, artemesia, statice,

bachelor buttons, and cockscomb. Many grasses and wildflowers also dry beautifully. Look for goldenrod, foxtail grass, and buttercups.

Early in the day, after the morning dew has burned off, set out for the garden or woods looking for blemish-free flowers that are not wet. Cut the stems long and remove any unsightly lower leaves. When you get home, tie the materials in bunches of six to ten stems with a piece of sisal or a rubber band. Hang them in a dry spot with good air circulation and not a lot of direct sunlight. Because drying times vary for flowers, check after one week. After that, check every few days.

Some flowers are better dried upright: Chinese lantern, baby's breath, and globe amaranth in particular. Stand them in a jar in a protected spot out of the way of breezes and direct sunlight. Other flowers should be slowly dried standing up in a jar with a small amount of water (1/2 inch) on the bottom. This method works well with yarrow, alliums, and hydrangeas. Pick long stemmed bouquets just as the blooms are starting to dry on the plant. As with any flowers you're drying, don't crowd the jar with too many stems.

I love the delicate look of Queen Anne's lace, but they always drooped as they dried. I finally hit on a method of drying the flowers with their heads supported by a small piece of wire screen (purchased in the hardware store). The screen must be elevated to allow air to dry the head. I punched a hole in the screen, inserted the stem, pulled the flower down until the head rested on the screen. Then I placed the screen atop four glasses; a few days later, I had a perfectly dried flower.

When you are going to be working with dried flowers, try to choose a warm, dry day, so that the flowers don't absorb moisture.

Dried herbs look beautiful in wreaths and are wonderful for cooking with in the heart of winter. Every wreath-maker should have lots of different kinds available: rosemary, sage, tarragon, and lemon thyme are among the best to dry. Harvest bunches in midsummer before the herbs flower and lose much of their vigor. Pick them early in the day when their oil content and flavor are at their peak. Tie them together in small bunches and hang them in a dark well-ventilated room for about two weeks.

If you experience trouble with flower heads falling off after drying, you may want to pre-wire the stems. This is easy to do with #22-gauge green floral wire. Cut off a piece of wire about 10 inches long. Trim the flower stems, leaving one to two inches. Insert the wire up the remaining stem into the flower head. Bend the top of the wire into a "U" shape and insert back into the flower head, but not through the stem. Wrap the flower stem and the wire stem with green floral tape. After the flower is dried, you can add a longer stem if necessary.

Heavier flowers, such as roses, need more support. Insert a 6-inch piece of floral wire crosswise through the bottom of the flower. After drying, you'll bend both ends of the wire down and cover with floral tape. Again, you can add a longer stem if necessary.

Some flowers such as roses and peonies are best dried buried in a substance that slowly draws the moisture out of them. For centuries, flowers were dried in sand, which is fairly effective for large heavy flowers. This method is very slow and the weight of the sand can damage delicate petals. However, if you're

dried pepper wreath

The classic dried pepper wreath can be made with different varieties of peppers: the authentic pobano or cayenne, Anaheim or Hungarian Wax. Gather the ripe peppers on a hot day and, if necessary, dry with paper towels. Thread a needle with a long piece of heavy thread then one by one, run the needle through the center of each pepper, leaving one inch between peppers. Hang in a warm, dry, dark, well-ventilated spot until they feel dry. Check frequently. You need between 75 and 100 dried peppers to make an 8-inch wreath.

staying at a beach house, and there's a plentiful supply of dahlias or peonies about, try this method. Pour a 1-inch layer of clean, dry sand in the bottom of large shoe box, add the flower, then very gently cover it with more sand. Tape the lid of the box with masking tape to keep out the air. Check for dryness in about two weeks.

For superior dried flowers, wreath-makers use silica gel. This substance resembles fine white sand, but it draws out moisture from flowers much more quickly, leaving vivid color and form. And silica gel is lightweight, so it doesn't damage delicate petals and leaves. Available in craft stores, silica gel does seem expensive at first, but it can be used over and over, spreading out its high start-up cost over time. Follow the directions on the package to reactivate it.

garlic wreath

A twist on the traditional garland of garlic is a hefty wreath of garlic. To make one, select full, firm garlic heads of a uniform size. Hot glue them onto a straw base covered with dainty white or lavender statice. Tuck springs of the statice between the garlic heads. If you can bear to dismantle the wreath to use the garlic, just pull of the heads, one by one; otherwise, the wreath should look good for a couple of months.

Silica gel must be used in airtight, large-bottomed plastic containers with lids, shoe boxes, or cartons securely sealed with masking tape. Just as with other flower-drying methods, gather flowers that are dry, unblemished, and in different stages of maturity.

For wreath-making, the stems will need to be pre-wired before they are dried.

To dry the flowers, pour a 1-inch layer of silica gel on the bottom of the container, add the flowers, then cover with more silica gel poured slowly in a gentle stream. Top with a 1-inch layer. Flowers with large flat heads such as black-eyed Susans, daisies, and mums should be placed in the containers head down. Those with heavy heads, such as roses, should be placed head up. Long spiked flowers like snapdragons, lily-of-the-valley, and bleeding heart should be placed on their sides. Check in three to four days for dryness by gently removing the flowers. If they are completely dry, you can brush off any excess silica gel with a small paintbrush.

The microwave oven can be credited with more than making meals in minutes; it's added a new time-saving element to flower drying. What formerly took days can now take minutes. Microwave drying is not foolproof, however. The variables are the particular oven, the moisture content of the flowers, and the size of the container. But once you've achieved success, you'll see deep fresh colorings you never imagined possible.

Pour a $1/2$-inch layer of silica gel in the bottom of a small microwave container. Since metal cannot be used in microwaves, you won't be pre-wiring the stems. Cut the stems down anyway to save space in the container. Place a flower on top of the silica gel, then gently fill in with more silica gel, covering the flower with at least $1/2$ inch of gel. Make sure there is headroom in the container of at least 2 inches. After drying, carefully wire the flowers. (I know people who insert wooden toothpicks crosswise through the bottom of the blooms to keep a hole open into which a wire can be threaded afterward.) Experiment with different drying times; start with 90 seconds for roses, 30 for pansies. Let

the flowers rest for 10 to 20 minutes before removing them from the container.

Many harvest wreaths call for the delicacy of dried fruits and vegetables. Don't overlook these additions to your wreath-making inventory. Artichokes and shucked miniature corn will air-dry on a rack in about two weeks. Slices of fruit look festive in holiday wreaths. To dry apple slices, cut them into $1/8$-inch slices, leaving the skins on. Soak for 20 minutes in a cup of lemon juice with $1/2$ tablespoon of salt. Remove and dry thoroughly. Place side by side on the rack of a 140-degree oven. Because this is a slow method of drying, the slices could be in the oven for hours. Check after one hour and look for a lovely, leathery finish. Remove and store in an airtight container until ready to use.

caring for your wreath

The wreaths you create are important. Taking care of them will extend their life span.

If you need to transport a wreath, handle it with care to ensure it arrives intact. Keep the wreath indoors while you prepare the vehicle. Place a box of heavy cardboard on the largest flat surface in the back of the car. Put folded newspaper on the bottom of the box and crushed sheets of tissue paper in the corners. (Tissue paper has proven itself invaluable for propping wreaths in place without pressing in on them.) Then gently carry the wreath from the house and lay it in the prepared carton. If the carton is large, and there's a possibility that the wreath will shift around, carefully add more crumpled tissue. A flat piece of tissue or a light piece of plastic protects the wreath from the elements.

Large plastic garbage bags are also useful in a pinch for transporting wreaths; lay a bag on its side, line the bottom with tissue or newspaper so the wreath does not slide on the plastic in case of sudden stops, then slip the wreath in. Some wreaths that have materials on both sides and thus cannot be set down, such as double-sided wreaths, can be transported hung from the handles or hooks on the inside roof of the car.

When selecting a site to hang the wreath, be realistic. Fragile dried-flower wreaths do not do well on a door or on the wall behind a door, by a coat closet, in a high traffic area, or any place where they'll get knocked about. Keep delicate larkspur and hydrangeas for a more protected spot. On a busy front door, hang wreaths that do not age quickly, nor shed on passersby. (Be sure to hang wreaths securely so that they're not dangling askew every time a visitor enters.)

Most wreaths do not flourish in a steady stream of sunlight. Preserved and pressed flowers, in particular, will fade quickly if over-exposed, as will many ribbons and fabrics.

Store non-ephemeral wreaths, such as those made from fabric or buttons, as you would clothing: in a bag with mothballs.

Don't forget to mist a fresh-flower wreath regularly with water.

chapter two

wreaths to welcome spring

Spring starts the four seasons of wreath-making. In this season that straddles winter and summer, begin with a Rosebud Heart made from materials you may have dried and kept for a project to make when blustery March winds howl at the door. Another wreath to make while contemplating the change of seasons is the Button Wreath. It requires delicacy and patience, but the result is of heirloom quality. This chapter ends with something green and fresh, just as the season does—a Living Herb Wreath. In between, you'll find ideas that exemplify the spirit of the season, such as a robust Pussy Willow Wreath.

As much as possible, harvest your own materials. An hour spent picking a bouquet of violets, bleeding hearts, and lilies-of-the-valley is time well spent, and you'll enjoy the fruits of your labor for a long time to come. Some of the ideas here may spark ideas of your own; as always, feel free to be creative and vary the projects. Make a wreath that resonates with personal meaning by using flowers taken from a bride's bouquet, graduation corsage, or Mother's Day gift.

Spring is the time also to plan a cutting garden: sow the seeds for future wreaths with plantings of herbs and flowers to preserve and press.

rosebud heart

As if sweet-smelling rosebuds weren't romantic enough on their own, here they are paired with an ensemble of heart-shaped twig bases. It wasn't all play, however; this demonstrates how a variety of looks can be created just by changing the quantity of rosebuds. Easy to attach with a hot glue gun, rosebuds can be purchased at craft stores and florists or harvested and dried at home (see Drying Flowers, page 33). When gathering rosebuds, look for ones of a similar size with a good shape.

1. The wreath will hang by the ribbon. Before beginning, iron out any wrinkles or creases on the ribbon with an iron set on "cool." Fold the ribbon in half lengthwise and lay the center of it over the point at the bottom of the heart, anchoring the ribbon with one hand (or tape it to the wreath with masking tape if you find this awkward). With the other hand, take the ribbon ends, bring them around the back of the point and slip them over the back and through the loop in front. Wind each ribbon around the two sides until you're near the crest of the heart, then bring the ends together in the back and tie in a knot. This knot becomes the hanger.

2. To attach the rosebuds, start by trimming any protruding stems. Place the rosebuds and base on a flat surface covered with a large sheet of newspaper. Before gluing on the buds, arrange them on the base in a design of your choice, then remove them to the paper, replicating the shape of the design on the paper to help guide your gluing. With the glue gun, squeeze a drop of glue on the bottom of a rosebud, then press onto the base. Use a pair of tweezers to make this easier. Hold in place until dry but don't squeeze the buds—they're brittle and can break off. Repeat with the remaining rosebuds, alternating sides as you go along. Cut away any glue threads with scissors.

one 5- or 6-inch heart-shaped wreath

dried rosebuds (quantity depends on design)

2 yards satin ribbon

hot glue gun with clear drying glue

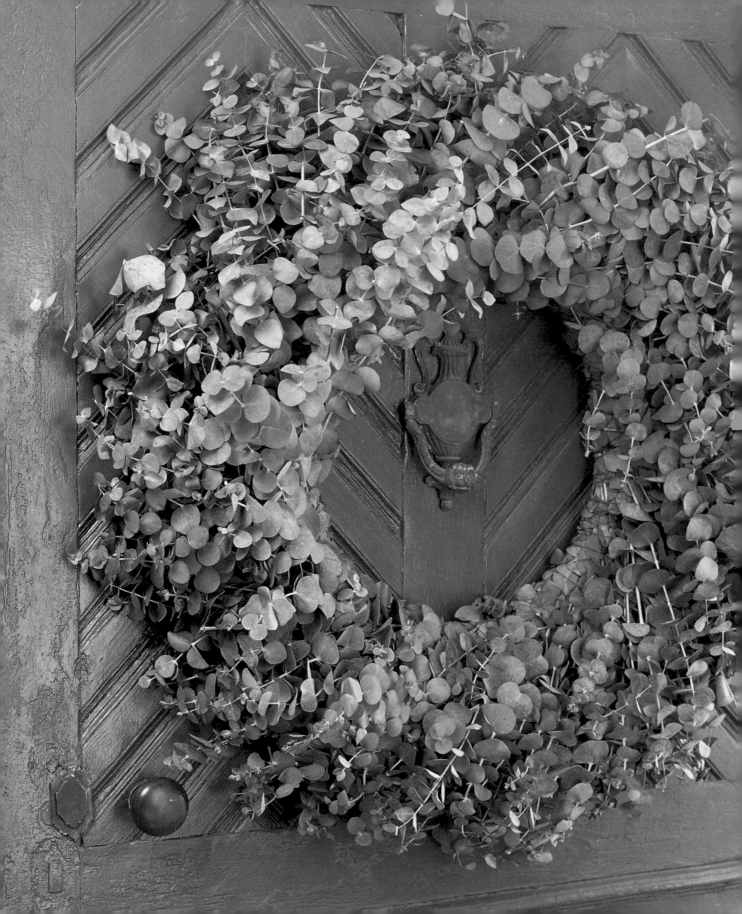

eucalyptus wreath

The invigorating scent of eucalyptus floats out every time you walk by this spectacular, oversized wreath. When complete, its wing span is more than 36 inches. While enormous wreaths are not usually displayed at close quarters, the scent is just too wonderful to miss. This wreath was made from fresh eucalyptus, which is supple and vastly easier to work with than dried. It ages to a glorious old age, its green-gray leaves muting to a silvery color and its fragrance lingering for months.

1. If making the base, shape the wire or coat hanger into a circle and twist both ends into loops. Hook the loops together, then close them with pliers, flattening the loops as much as possible.

2. To make a hanger, cut four 8-inch pieces of floral wire, then twist them together to form one piece. Knot both ends to the back of the base, forming a loop.

3. If you are using long uncut branches, separate the stems. Create clusters of stems; you'll need approximately 16 clusters to form the wreath. For each cluster, take 12 or 13 stems and tightly wrap the bottom 5 inches of the stems several times with floral wire. Leave on as many lower leaves as possible.

4. Attach a paddle of floral wire to the base. Place the first cluster next to the inside of the base and angle it out over the outside edge. Wrap the wire tightly around the stems several times, covering about 4 to 5 inches. Do not cut the wire. Take another cluster and overlap the first, placing it 3 to 4 inches down from the top of the previous one. Wire it onto the base. Repeat until the base is covered. Attach the last cluster by gently lifting up the top of the first and wiring on the stems of the last underneath it. Cut the wire.

one 16-inch-diameter wire ring base made of #16-gauge wire or 1 wire coat hanger

200 single stems of fresh eucalyptus cut 14 to 18 inches long, or 25 uncut branches, each with about 8 long stems

2 paddles #20-gauge green floral wire

button wreath

When things are just too beautiful to be tucked away in a drawer, it's time to make a wreath. This Button Wreath was inspired by a sister's immense button collection. Her dilemma: how could she display her treasures without actually using them? The solution: sew them on a wreath of creamy satin. This wreath would make a lovely frame, perhaps positioned around an old Victorian studio portrait.

1. To make the oval-shaped base, use the inner ring of the embroidery hoop. Pad it with fiber filling: first, tightly knot the end of the spool of thread onto the hoop. Then take a small handful of the fiber filling and mound it around the hoop. Wrap the thread around the filling several times. Keep adding filling until you have evenly covered the hoop. Try to keep it consistent to avoid lumps. The padded hoop should measure about 7 x 10 inches.

2. Before working with the ribbon, iron out any wrinkles or creases in the ribbon with an iron set on "cool." At the back of the base top, anchor the ribbon to the base with the dressmaker's pin at a point 18 inches in from the end of the ribbon. This excess ribbon will make the knot. Wrap the rest of the ribbon around the base, keeping the spacing even. Where the two ends meet at the top of the base, tie twice in a simple knot, letting the strands stream down the back or sides of the base. Remove the pin.

3. Using a long piece of thread, sew on the buttons one by one, starting with the inner circle. Don't knot the thread after each button, just go in each hole four to five times, then move on to the next. Consistency is important here; try to keep the holes facing in the same direction and the spacing even. Hang by the knotted ribbon.

one 8-inch oval embroidery hoop

thirty-five to forty 3/4-inch dark mother-of-pearl buttons

twenty-three to twenty-eight 3/4-inch white mother-of-pearl buttons

one small package fiber filling (found in the pillow section of craft stores)

one spool cream thread

4 yards 2 1/4-inch cream-colored satin ribbon

1 straight dressmaker's pin

lavender **wreath**

The gray-green foliage and small lavender flowers of the perennial Lavendula *plant have long made it one of the loveliest plants in the garden. With its long spikes spilling over a border, lavender arrives in late spring to scent the air with its intoxicating fragrance. One of the mainstays of aromatherapy, lavender is thought to cure a host of minor ailments. Kept in a dry place, this spectacular wreath will look—and smell—beautiful throughout the year.*

1. If making the base, shape the wire or coat hanger into a circle and twist both ends into loops. Hook the loops together, then close them with pliers, flattening the loops as much as possible.

2. To make a hanger, cut four 10-inch pieces of floral wire, then twist them together to form one piece. Knot both ends to the back of the base, forming a loop.

3. Make clusters of the lavender by taking 20 to 30 spikes and wrapping the bottom 4 inches of the stems together with the floral wire.

4. Cover the base with green floral tape. Attach the paddle of wire to the base. To attach the lavender, lay the bottom of the first cluster next to the inside ring, and angle out the top. Wrap the wire around the stems several times, covering about 3 or 4 inches of stem. Do not cut the wire. Take another cluster and overlap the first, placing it about 2 to 3 inches down from the top of the previous one. Continue adding clusters until the base is covered. Attach the last cluster by gently lifting up the top of the first and wiring on the stems of the last underneath it. Cut the wire.

one 14-inch-diameter wire ring base made of #16-gauge wire or 1 wire coat hanger

300 to 400 spikes dried lavender

1 paddle #22-gauge green floral wire

1 roll green floral tape

pussy willow
wreath

One of the earliest blooms to greet us in spring, the catkins on pussy willow are always a welcome sight. If you're impatient for blooms, gather branches any time after New Year's Day to force indoors. Crush the stems with a hammer, then plunge them into a bucket of warm water. In two weeks or less, you'll be rewarded with dozens of newly-opening buds. Be sure to gather extra for bouquets around the house.

1. To make the base, tie together the stems of the 6-foot branches with floral wire. Hold the ends in one hand and with the other form a circle about 14 inches in diameter. Secure the branches with a short piece of floral wire. Continue forming the base with the branches, weaving in the ends and keeping an eye on the balance of the buds.

2. To make a hanger at the top of the base back, cut four 10-inch pieces of floral wire, then twist them together to form one piece. Knot both ends to the back of the base, forming a loop.

3. Take the shorter pussy willow branches and divide them into 20 clusters, mixing the lengths for a random look. Tightly wrap the bottom 5 inches of the stems several times with floral wire.

4. Attach the paddle of floral wire to the base. Place a cluster on the base and wire it on, wrapping the stems several times. Do not cut the wire. Take another cluster and overlap the first, placing it about 6 inches down from the top of the previous one. Wire it onto the base. Continue adding clusters until the base is covered. Attach the last cluster by gently lifting the first cluster and wiring on the stems of the last underneath it. Cut the wire.

2 branches pussy willow cut 6 feet long

20 branches pussy willow cut 24 inches long

20 branches pussy willow cut 18 inches long

20 branches pussy willow cut 12 inches long

1 paddle #22-gauge green floral wire

living herb & flower **wreath**

A glorious way to say good-bye to spring and usher in summer, a Living Herb & Flower Wreath groans with dewy herbs and late spring flowers. Make it from the herbs you cook with most often and hang it near a sunny kitchen door. You'll be blessed with fresh herbs all summer long, not to mention clouds of intoxicating scents. Nearly any herb can be used. Try to contrast textures—such as spiky rosemary with mats of thyme— and colors—yellowy lemon thyme with purplish basil. Perky violas add a dash of humor.

1. Thoroughly saturate the moss, then wring out the excess water. Lay the chicken wire down and place the moss on top in a strip down the middle. Carefully fold over the wire into a tube 54 inches long. Bend the tube into a circle and, where the ends meet, lace the wire together with pliers.

2. This wreath will be heavy and requires a strong hanger. Make one by cutting five 24-inch long pieces of floral wire, then twist them together. Knot both ends to the back of the base, forming a loop.

3. Lay the base down and arrange the flowers and herbs on top to get a general idea of the design. Remove the plants.

4. Using the pliers, clip openings in the chicken wire large enough for the plants, and tamp down the moss to accommodate the soil balls. Hang the base at display height, then add the plants. Secure the plants through the chicken wire with U-shaped floral pins. As the plants grow, they will completely cover the wreath. Be sure to water well every few days and drain before re-hanging, otherwise the wreath will be excessively heavy.

one 10 x 54-inch piece chicken wire

2 large bags sphagnum moss

a selection of herbs in small pots or starter packs from the nursery: tarragon, thyme, rosemary, oregano, basil

4 small pots or starter packs of violas

needle-nosed pliers with cutter

1 paddle #22-gauge green floral wire

1 package U-shaped floral pins

chapter two

summertime wreaths

Summer arrives with a blast of heat and a show of color. For the wreath-maker, it's prime time. Flowers bloom from seeds and cuttings planted in the early spring. The perennial border overflows with interesting specimens to preserve and dry for wreath-making. Plump heads of blue hydrangea burst into color in July and it seems as though the cutting scissors can't fly fast enough.

While it's wonderful to marry any time of the year, June still remains the most popular wedding month. In this chapter, you'll learn how to make a romantic Bridal Wreath, entwined with fresh roses. You can make this wreath in any season with roses from the florist, or you can dash out into the garden early on a wedding morn to clip a couple dozen.

The wreath-maker is always on the go now. Long walks result in wildflower bouquets waiting to be preserved. Fresh flowers can be dried so that their colors, shapes, and textures remain alive in wreaths. Herbs and flowers can be combined for spectacular effects, as in an opulent wreath of artemesia or in a glorious sphere dominated by fresh sage. With their findings, beachcombers can create a long-lasting memory of hot summer days.

seashell wreath

Collecting seashells on vacation is lots of fun, especially for children who delight in every thrilling discovery. Once home, a beautiful way to bring back the holiday feeling is with a Seashell Wreath. Rather than being arranged symmetrically, an abundance of clam shells, scallop shells, cockles, angel wings, sea pens, and arc wings jostle next to each other, just as they would at the shore. A plywood base provides support while letting the wreath lay flat.

1. Attach the metal hanger at the top of the base back. Spray both sides of the base with several coats of paint, making sure to cover the inside and outside rims. Allow to dry thoroughly between coats and before continuing.

2. Divide the shells into piles by color, size, shape, and texture (even a random, just-washed-ashore look requires a bit of organization). Pick out 12 similarly sized shells and with the hot glue gun, glue them three-in-a-row at 12, 3, 6, and 9 o'clock on the outer rim of the base. Next, edge the inside with a row of scallop shells and glue them on.

3. Hang the wreath at display height. Glue on the remaining shells. To make "oyster shells," glue down one shell, glue a pearl inside it, then position a matching shell on top of it so it looks as if the "oyster" were opening, revealing a pearl within.

one 18-inch-diameter wooden base of 3/8- to 1/2-inch plywood (our base has a 4-inch band with an inner circle of 10 inches)

seashells (at least 5 cups or one large sand-pail full)

1 metal picture hanger (for 5- to 10-lb. weight)

1 can coral-colored spray paint (fast-drying kind)

hot glue gun with 5 or 6 long clear glue sticks

3 pearl beads (optional)

variation

For a real sandy shores feeling, instead of spray painting the wreath base, cover it with sand. Working in small sections, spread on a thin coat of clear-drying glue. While the glue is wet, sprinkle clean sand over it. When completely dry, glue on the shells with a glue gun.

hydrangea wreath

The vivid blue blooms of Hydrangea macrophylla *are the result of an acid soil. Blooming in the mid-summer, this extraordinary flower plays the lead role in a wreath accented by tiny clusters of pink and lavender-colored* Hydrangea paniculata *(which usually appears in late fall). Both are well worth waiting for and drying; for a lush wreath, you will need an abundance of flowers. This beautiful wreath will last at least a year.*

1. To be able to assemble this wreath at display height, make a hanger by wrapping floral wire around the top of the base several times Cut the wire and knot the ends tightly. Cut three 6-inch lengths of wire, then twist them together to form one piece. Slip the twisted wire under the wire attached to the base and knot the ends together, forming a loop at the back of the base.

2. Dried hydrangea flowers are delicate and need to be wired with care onto floral picks for insertion into the straw base. Place the top of the hydrangea stem next to the top of the pick and wrap the attached wire around both. Do this for all of the hydrangea heads.

3. Hang the wreath at display height. Leaving a 3-inch wide space for the ribbon bow, insert the wooden picks into the base, starting at the top. Push them in firmly, but carefully, so as not to bruise or break the flowers. Continue placing the clusters, making sure to cover both the outside and the inside of the base. Distribute the flowers so that there are not too many in one spot, and so that the wreath looks balanced.

4. Around the space at the top where you left the opening, bend back the wire hanger, then wrap the ribbon around the base and tie it into a bow, or make a knot in the ribbon about a foot above the wreath and hang it from a hook.

---

one 14-inch-diameter rounded straw base

24 to 36 dried blue hydrangea heads and some purple/pink heads

1 paddle #22-gauge green floral wire

1 package green wired wooden floral picks

2 yards lavender-colored, 3-inch wide wired ribbon

porch wreath

Bring the beauty of the garden up close with this simple but captivating wreath. Inside its pockets, you can tuck a palm-size garden of pansies in April and May, dianthus in June, daisies in July and August, mums in the fall. Flowering house plants, such as African violets or tiny oxalis would also work, and think how comforting crocus, lily-of-the-valley, and other forced bulbs would look in the depths of winter. This one is filled with Johnnie-jump-ups. Vary the basket sizes to accommodate the flowers of your choice, and remember to water frequently.

1. Make a hanging loop by cutting five 12-inch lengths of floral wire and twisting them together. Knot both ends to the top of the back of the base, forming a loop. Be sure to tie the wires firmly through several sturdy branches.

2. Lay the base on a flat surface and position the baskets so that they are an equal distance apart. Attach them by weaving foot-long lengths of floral wire through each basket and the base in several different places along the top and bottom of the baskets.

3. Hang the base at display height and check that all the baskets are firmly attached and straight. Tear off chunks of moss and push them into the pockets of the baskets. Thoroughly water the plants. Cover each soil ball with a small piece of plastic wrap, then place one plant in each basket. Hang the wreath where it will not be exposed to prolonged sunlight and gusts of wind, and water the plants often.

one 20-inch-diameter vine wreath base

8 Johnnie-jump-up plants

4 clumps garden moss

1 paddle #22-gauge green floral wire

8 baskets

plastic wrap

containers

Craft stores offer a selection of containers that would work equally well here. Small terra cotta "half" pots would be charming and will keep the plants moist longer than the baskets do.

bridal wreath

If ever there is an occasion to go all out, it's a wedding. This joyous wreath of fresh roses dazzles passersby and could welcome guests when hung on a front door or mark off a place of honor on the back of the bride's chair. Roses hold up surprisingly well out of water and will stay vibrant for several hours if kept out of direct sunlight.

1. If making the wire base, shape the wire or hanger into a circle and twist both ends into loops. Hook the loops together, then close them with pliers, flattening the loops as much as possible. Cover the entire base with green floral tape. From the paddle of green floral wire, cut 48 pieces of wire, each about 8 inches long.

2. Working with two roses at a time (keep the others in water), cut the stems to about 4 inches long. Do not discard the stems; instead, remove each cluster of leaves. Place two clusters of leaves and one short piece of astilbe next to two roses and wrap them together with a piece of pre-cut floral wire. Attach one end of the paddle of floral wire to the base. Now, position the cluster next to the base, with its head extending slightly over the outer edge. Wrap the paddle of wire all the way down the cluster stem, pulling it tightly to secure. Do not cut the wire. Prepare another rose, leaf, and astilbe cluster and place it close to the first, concealing the stem of the previous cluster. Fill in any uneven spots with clusters of rose and astilbe leaves. Continue adding flowers, evenly spaced all around the wire base, until the base is completely covered.

one 16-inch-diameter wire ring base made of #16-gauge wire or 1 wire coat hanger

48 fresh roses with their leaves

1 bunch astilbe, about 6 stems

pliers

1 roll green floral tape

1 paddle #22-gauge green floral wire

variation

Use seasonal flowers: daffodils and muscari in spring; dianthus, bachelor buttons, daisies, and baby's breath in summer; dahlias, mums, and marigolds in fall. For a winter wedding, orchids would be ravishing.

dried wildflower wreath

Welcome guests with the sights of a summer meadow by hanging a dried wildflower wreath on the front door. Wildflowers, grasses, and seeds grow along roadsides, abandoned lots, and meadows. Look for thickets of wild roses, stands of foxtail grass, Queen Anne's lace, goldenrod, feverfew, milkweed, rabbit tobacco, wild yarrow, teasel, Sweet Annie, and daisies. Don't overlook pods, clover, and thistle. Try to gather as lush an assortment as possible. One caution: be sure you are welcome to gather wildflowers; some areas are protected and do not permit picking.

1. To make a hanger, wrap floral wire around the top of the base in one spot several times. Cut the wire and knot the ends tightly. Cut three 8-inch pieces of wire, then twist them together to form one piece. Slip the twisted wire under the wire attached to the base and knot the ends together, forming a loop at the back of the base.

2. Cover the base with handfuls of sphagnum moss attached with U-shaped floral pins.

3. Working with dried flowers on a warm, dry day is best as the flowers don't absorb moisture. Make clusters by gathering four or five stems and attaching them to a floral pick. Insert the clusters into the base. Try to work in one direction and from the inside of the wreath to the outside. Attach the last cluster by gently lifting up the head of the first.

one 10-inch-diameter straw wreath base

assorted dried wildflowers and grasses (at least 24 bunches of 4 or 5 botanicals each plus individual specimen plants)

1 bag sphagnum moss

1 paddle #22-gauge green floral wire

1 bag U-shaped floral pins

1 package green wired wooden floral picks

artemesia wreath

With its clouds of silver foliage, artemesia is a staple of dried flower wreaths. As a background for darker flowers and herbs, this feathery, shrubby plant is hard to beat. Technically an herb, fragrant flowers appear on many varieties in late summer. It's mixed here with rusty arctostaphylos *(manzanita), which dries beautifully, and bright red pepperberries.*

1. To make a hanger, wrap floral wire around the base in one spot several times. Cut the wire and knot the ends tightly. Cut three 10-inch pieces of wire; then twist them together to form one piece. Slip the twisted wire under the wire attached to the base and knot the ends together, forming a loop at the back of the base.

2. To cover the base with the artemesia, make clusters of 5 stems each. Wrap the bottom of the stems with the floral wire. Then attach each one to a floral pick. Insert the picks around the base starting near the inside of the ring, and pointing all the bunches outward in the same direction. To attach the last bunch, gently lift the top of the first and insert the last underneath it.

3. Make clusters of the arctostaphylos by wiring together three stems with the wire on the end of the floral pick. Retain as many leaves as possible. Insert at regular intervals on the base.

4. Wire each pepperberry stem to a floral pick and insert at regularly spaced intervals. Gently lift some of the artemesia every now and then and insert pepperberries underneath for a more natural look.

one 18-inch-diameter straw wreath base

5 large bunches dried artemesia cut 8 to 10 inches long

3 dozen dried arctostaphylos (with leaves) cut 6 inches long

12 stems of pepperberries cut 8 inches long

1 paddle #22-gauge green floral wire

2 packages green wired wooden floral picks

sage wreath

Hanging from a weather-beaten fence, or inside by the hearth, a plump wreath of aromatic sage will insure wonderful dining throughout the fall and winter months. To make this lush wreath, try to obtain a source (perhaps a local nursery) for sage still on the branch. If you wish to dry this wreath, lay it on a flat surface in a dark dry room for about two weeks.

1. Make a hanging loop for the base by cutting three 10-inch lengths of floral wire and twisting them together into one. Insert the wire into the top ring on the back and form it into a 5-inch circle. Coil the ends around the circle.

2. Make clusters of mixed herbs by wiring together the stems of about six sprigs in a bundle. Repeat with the yarrow and the lamb's ears. Attach the paddle of floral wire to the base. Lay an herb cluster down on the base, with its top angled out, and wind the wire around the stems several times. Do not cut the wire. Take another cluster of herbs and, with its top angled in, overlap the first, placing it about 5 inches down from the top of the first cluster and concealing its stems. Wire it to the base. Continue adding clusters of herbs until the base is covered, alternating the angle of the clusters. Attach the last cluster by gently lifting up the top of the first cluster and wiring on the stems of the last. Do not cut the wire.

3. Lay a cluster of lamb's ears and a cluster of yarrow atop the previous herb stems and wire onto the base. Continue by wiring on two clusters of herbs, then one cluster of yarrow and lamb's ears, until the base is covered. When done, cut the wire.

one 12-inch-diameter wire box frame

124 sprigs of fresh herbs: sage, oregano, or thyme, cut 7 inches long

bunch of white yarrow (at least 12 stems)

lamb's ears (at least 12 stems) cut 5 inches long

1 paddle #22-gauge green floral wire

2 packages green wired wooden floral picks

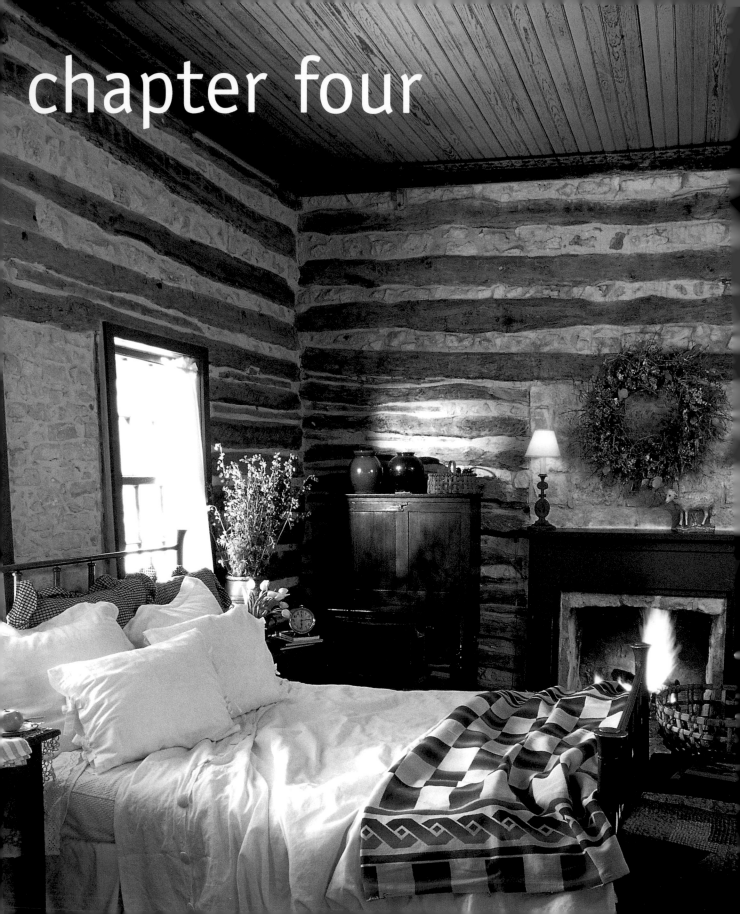

chapter four

wreaths from the harvest

Autumn is a season of opportunity for the wreath-maker. The flower garden blooms until the first hard frost, giving us sunflowers, marigolds, zinnias, globe amaranth, mums, strawflowers, and more. The herb garden is still going strong with lush mounds of sage, parsley, rosemary, basil, thyme, marjoram, and bay leaves—all of which look wonderful on wreaths dried and fresh. The fields yield up their crops and everywhere there are displays of materials for wreaths. Baskets of fall leaves, bright with color, can be sorted for glorious wreaths.

When the farm stands start hanging up bunches of Indian corn, an autumn tradition, hang up an Indian corn wreath, your own homage to the harvest. Children can help gather up chili peppers for a wreath, or gourds and miniature pumpkins for a harvest wreath. Clip strands of bittersweet vine and make a stunning wreath in minutes.

Toward the end of fall, activity moves inside and the whole house becomes a backdrop for decoration. Acorns, nuts, and berries come out of bags to be sorted and made into wreaths that complement the snugness of quilts and hooked rugs. It is a time to celebrate the earth's bounty.

pinecone heart wreath

No fall would be complete without creating a classic pinecone wreath. And so, on a late afternoon, my daughter and I set out to look for interesting specimens. Our efforts were quickly rewarded. Just around the corner, under an old pine tree that shelters the manse of the local church, scores of miniature pinecones spilled into the street. Out came the collecting bag, and home we went with a treasure that we later happily dried and sorted—wondering why we had never before noticed these charming objects literally under our feet.

1. To highlight a pretty ribbon, we let much of it show. Before beginning, iron out any wrinkles or creases on the ribbon with an iron set on "cool." To attach the ribbon, fold the ribbon in half lengthwise and lay the center of it over the point at the bottom of the heart, anchoring the ribbon with one hand (or tape it to the wreath with masking tape if you find this awkward). With the other hand, take the ribbon ends, bring them around the back of the point and slip them over the back and through the loop in front. Wind each ribbon around the two sides until you're near the crest of the heart, then bring the two ends together in the back and make a knot about 18 inches away from the base. This knot becomes the hanger.

2. Hang the base at display height. With the hot glue gun, glue on the pinecones one by one. Hold in place until dry. (Don't use too much glue, to avoid drips.) Cluster the pinecones heavily on the top of the heart and at the bottom point. In between, make two smaller clusters on each side of the heart.

one 12-inch heart-shaped vine wreath

5 to 6 dozen small pinecones

4 yards 2-inch wide tartan ribbon

hot glue gun and clear glue sticks

masking tape (optional)

bittersweet vine **wreath**

Come autumn, the countryside is alive with the twining stems of Celastrus, *more commonly known as bittersweet. Spilling over stone walls and making itself at home nearly everywhere, bittersweet is a rampant grower whose stock you need not worry about depleting. Its wild tendrils and fiery berries are so eye-catching that the wreath needs no embellishment at all. This wreath will last through the fall and winter. Take care where you display it, however; the vine tends to drop its berries, which are poisonous, so do not hang it up near areas that will stain, or where children play unsupervised.*

1. Bittersweet, like all vines, is easiest to work with when it is supple. Wait until after a good rain storm to collect your branches and make this wreath.

2. Since bittersweet is nearly impossible to contort into a clean round shape, go with its unruly quality and let it be the boss. There are different ways to form a wreath: one is to hold an end of a long branch in one hand and, with the other hand, form a circle the size you want. (You can fasten the base with a small piece of floral wire if it's difficult to hold.) Continue forming the base with the branch, weaving in the end to secure. As one branch ends, insert a new branch into the wreath and keep adding more until you form the size of wreath you want.

3. Another technique is to take several branches of the vine, tie the ends together with floral wire, then twist them into a circle the size you want. Tie with floral wire. Wrap the remainder of the vine around the "base," tucking in the ends as you go along. Weave in more branches, one by one, as needed. If one side is skimpier than the other, insert the end of a new branch and transplant more in. Hang with a piece of paper ribbon, tied in a loop.

5 to 10 branches bittersweet, cut 3 to 4 feet long

one 1-inch piece #22-gauge green floral wire (optional)

12 inches rusty-red paper ribbon

indian corn wreath

Country produce stands, nurseries, and green markets fill up with the fruits of the harvest every autumn, including Indian corn, usually hung on the front door. Adapt this old American custom by creating a wreath made from dozens of ears of miniature corn. Apart from its important symbolic value, to the wreath-maker Indian corn—with its radiant jewellike kernels and blazing palette—is visually exciting material. If you hang this wonderful wreath outside, the birds will thank you as they feast on it over the winter.

1. A note of warning: making this base is messy, so it's best to work on a newspaper-covered surface. Start by attaching a hanger to the top of the base back. Cut a 14-inch length of sisal twine and tightly knot it in a loop to the top ring on the frame. To cover the frame with straw, attach the end of the paddle of floral wire to the frame, then take a generous handful of straw, lay it on the frame, and wrap the wire around it at about 1-inch intervals. Do not cut the wire. Continue adding straw and wrapping with wire until the frame is completely covered. Cut the wire. Wrap the sisal twine around the base frame once and knot it. Do not cut the twine. Continue wrapping it around the frame at 2-inch intervals. Knot the end in the last loop.

2. If the husks on the ears of corn are wrinkled or misshapen, run them under hot water for a minute or two, then re-shape; to keep the husks of each ear together, tie them with a small piece of twine. Arrange the ears of corn around the base, then remove them to a piece of newspaper, keeping the design intact. Hang the base at display height. With the hot glue gun, dab a ribbon of glue on the back of an ear of corn and press it down firmly. Repeat until the entire front of the base has been covered with corn.

one 18-inch-diameter wire frame box

40 to 45 ears miniature Indian corn

1 bale craft straw

1 spool sisal twine

1 paddle #22-gauge green floral wire

hot glue gun and clear glue sticks

country wheat
wreath

While we may think of the wheat wreath as a traditional American custom, its roots go further back in time. Over 2,500 years ago, in the ancient Greek and Roman civilizations, men and women were married wearing crowns of wheat, a symbol of fertility. Today, wheat remains a symbol of the harvest—and that's why this Country Wheat Wreath couldn't' be more appropriate. Combining wheat and oats gives a nicely textured wreath, will last for as long as you want to keep it.

1. If making the base, shape the wire or coat hanger into a circle and twist both ends into loops. Hook the loops together, then close them with pliers, flattening the loops as much as possible.

2. Make a hanging loop for the back of the base by cutting two 6-inch lengths of floral wire and twisting them together. Knot each end on the base, forming a loop.

3. Prepare the wheat and oat stalks by laying them in neat piles, keeping the bottoms lined up and facing the same direction. Cut the ends so the stalks are about 12 inches long. Make clusters of about 30 mixed stalks, and tightly wrap the bottom 4 inches of the stems several times with the floral wire. You'll need 50 to 60 clusters.

4. Attach the paddle of floral wire to the base. Place a cluster on the frame. Wrap the stems tightly with the wire several times, covering about 5 inches. Do not cut the wire. Take another cluster and overlap the first, placing it about 5 inches down from the top of the previous one. Wire onto the base. Keep the spacing consistent and repeat until you have completed the wreath. Attach the last cluster by gently lifting the top of the first and wiring on the stems of the last underneath it. Cut the wire.

one 8-inch-diameter wire ring base made of #16-gauge wire or 1 wire coat hanger

¼ bushel dried wheat stalks

¼ bushel dried oat stalks

1 paddle #22-gauge green floral wire

harvest wreath

Heavy with bittersweet, miniature pumpkins, and gourds, this bountiful wreath is a fitting tribute to the conclusion of a successful growing season. Hung by the garden gate, or on a wall outside the house, the ever-chillier nights of fall keep it fresh for many weeks.

1. To make a base of bittersweet and grapevine, form the four 6-foot grapevine branches into a 24-inch circle. Hold the circle together with one hand, or tie with floral wire.

2. Take one 3-foot grapevine branch and tightly wrap it around the circle, forming coiled loops about 4 to 5 inches apart. Weave in the end. Insert the remaining grapevine branch, and wrap it in the same way.

3. Working with one bittersweet branch at a time, weave an end into the base. Form the same coils as you did with the grapevine, weaving in the ends.

4. To make a hanger at the top of the back, cut four 10-inch long pieces of floral wire, then twist them to form one piece. Knot both ends to the back of the base, forming a loop.

5. Attach the pumpkins and gourds using the floral picks. Insert the picks into the fruit, then secure to a sturdy part of the base with the wire.

4 grapevine branches cut 6 feet long

2 grapevine branches cut 3 feet long

6 bittersweet branches cut 1 to 2 feet long

12 miniature gourds

12 miniature pumpkins

1 paddle #22-gauge green floral wire

1 package green wired wooden floral picks

variation

Embellish this wreath—or substitute the gourds—with other fruits of the harvest. Small apples, squashes, and Indian corn can be attached to the base with wooden floral picks.

bay leaves, nuts &
hawthorn berries wreath

A study in scarlet—the bay window in this festive kitchen is the perfect staging area for a lush wreath of bay leaves, nuts, and hawthorn berries. The aromatic leaves of the bay lace the air with their light scent while the bright red berries on the hawthorn branches make a fine show. An assortment of nuts adds color and shine to a wreath that couldn't be more natural. You may have to visit a nursery or garden speciality store for bay leaves on branches.

1. Make a hanger for the back of the base by cutting five 14-inch pieces of floral wire and twisting them together into one. Insert through the back of the base about 3 inches down from the top. Knot the ends together, coiling the excess around the hanging loop.

2. Attach the paddle of floral wire to the base. Lay down a branch of bay leaves on the frame and wire the lower stem to the base. Do not cut the wire. Take a second branch of bay leaves and overlap the first, placing it about 3 inches down from the top of the previous one. Wire onto the base. Continue adding branches of bay leaves until the base is covered. Attach the last branch by gently lifting the top of the first and wiring on the stem of the last underneath it. Cut the wire.

3. Attach the hawthorn berries to the wired wooden picks by laying a stem next to the pick and winding the wire around the stem. Arrange them evenly around the base, then insert the picks into the frame.

4. Using the hot glue gun, glue on the nuts. Remember, full wreaths are best, so add a generous amount.

one 18-inch-diameter vine wreath base

20 bay leaf branches, cut 18 inches long

12 hawthorn berry stems, cut 14 inches long

2 cups assorted nuts

1 paddle #22-gauge green floral wire

1 package green wired wooden floral picks

hot glue gun and clear glue sticks

chapter five

cold weather wreaths

To some winter may present a challenge. But not to the wreath-maker. This is a season of glory and joy, meant to be enjoyed to its fullest. There isn't a spot inside or outside the home that doesn't deserve a wreath. Outdoors, adorn a barn door with a twig wreath. To greet friends, enliven the front door with a Pomegranate and Ivy Wreath, a traditional American wreath. Indoors, the air is heavy with the scent of baking as dozens of gingerbread boys emerge from the oven in time for their appearance on a Gingerbread Boy Wreath.

Winter is also the time of year to bring the outdoors in with baskets of material gathered from the garden and woods. Fir, boxwood, pinecones, and grapevine are snipped by the armful. Festive to look at, they're natural decorations that need little embellishment. But when you want to pull out all the stops, make an heirloom project that will be enjoyed year after year: a Jingle Bell Wreath or a gold-clad Pinecone Wreath.

Some wreaths are given as gifts, others embellish a gift, like the satin-wrapped Cameo Gift Wreath. Just the right size for a mantle, an Ivy Topiary Wreath adds its own presence to the holidays, then stays on to become a sprightly sight over the winter.

ivy & pomegranate
wreath

Bright red pomegranates appear during the winter holidays. Enjoy their delectable jewellike fruit, then use the shells for this festive wreath. Position the pomegranate halves any way you desire, or follow this design. This wreath stays fresh-looking for up to ten days, then fades into lovely, leathery old age.

1. Soak the sphagnum moss according to the package directions. Wring out excess water and distribute the damp moss evenly on the front of the base. Attach the moss by winding the paddle of floral wire around the base in circles about 1 inch apart. Twist the two ends of the wire together where they meet up at the back of the base.

2. To make a hanger, cut five 12-inch pieces of floral wire, then twist them together to form one piece. Knot both ends to sturdy vine branches on the back of the base, forming a loop.

3. To attach the pomegranates, cut each one in half and remove the fruit. Using the precut lengths of #16-gauge floral wire, pierce each pomegranate half at a twelve o'clock and six o'clock position, about 1 inch from the cut edge. Thread the wires through the holes. Arrange the eight halves on the base, then remove them, leaving a marker where you want each to be. One by one, attach the halves by twisting the wires together in the back to secure.

4. Attach clusters of ivy to the floral picks by wrapping the stems with the attached wire. Push the picks into the moss evenly over all the base, aiming to cover the inner and outer edges. Sprinkle the moss with water every day to prolong the life of the wreath.

one 20-inch-diameter vine wreath base

one 16-ounce bag sphagnum moss

4 large, unblemished pomegranates

18 to 20 sprigs of variegated ivy

eight 18-inch pieces #16-gauge floral wire

1 paddle #22-gauge green floral wire

1 package wired wooden floral picks

grapevine wreath

Whether growing in the wild or spilling over a trellis, fence, or arbor, grapevines are a pleasure to watch grow. Serious gardeners train their vines into different shapes to improve grape production, pruning away old canes each winter. Use these canes to make a wreath. A generous friend bought a country house complete with abandoned grapevines and I was fortunate to be there, pruners in hand, on a blustery November afternoon to gather old canes for this wreath. This and the Bittersweet Vine Wreath are the two easiest natural wreaths to make. Not surprisingly, the techniques are nearly the same.

1. Grape branches are best to work with when freshly cut or damp; otherwise, they can become brittle. Before making this wreath, let the branches sit outside in a soaking rain or hose them down. Try not to break off any of the tendrils, which give the wreath so much character.

2. Clasping three or four branches in your hand at once, twist the branches to form a circular shape or "base," 24 inches in diameter. (You can fasten the base with the small piece of sisal if it's difficult to hold the branches.) Continue by coiling the branches around the base, forming loops 4 to 5 inches apart. Weave in the ends to conceal them. Add more branches one at a time, weaving and coiling them in until you have the fullness you want. Grapevine is supple and any stray branches or tendrils can be easily tucked in between the circles. This wreath requires no hanger and will slip easily over a hook.

6 to 10 grape canes (grapevine branches), cut 6 to 8 feet long

one 10-inch length sisal twine (optional)

variation

The natural look of a grapevine wreath blends nicely with other elements that also celebrate the season: mistletoe, rose hips, and holly. Try tying them with plaid or checkered ribbon.

gingerbread boy wreath

With recipes dating back to the 1300s, gingerbread is thought to be the oldest sweet confection, and it has been a part of Christmas celebrations for generations. This merry wreath can be made from your favorite recipe and cut into whatever forms please you.

1. Before baking, cut two holes in the "bellies" of the gingerbread boys to make buttonholes (a chopstick does this nicely). Try to make extra cookies in case of mishaps. After baking, remove the cookies from the baking tray and let cool and harden completely, overnight or longer.

2. Spray the wreath base with several light coats of gold paint. Allow the paint to dry completely between coats.

3. To make the ribbon "buttonholes": cut the ⅛-inch wide ribbon in 14 pieces, each 11 inches long. Fold each piece in half. On the wrong side of the cookies, poke the fold of one ribbon through the lower buttonhole just until the ribbon shows. Then place both strands of the ribbon between the holes and secure them with a dab of hot glue. Push the folds through the top buttonhole the same way you did the bottom. Bring both strands out on the cookie "neck" and secure with hot glue.

4. Preview the wreath by placing the cookies on the base to be sure they fit; leave about 1½ inches of space for the wired ribbon. Put a cookie on the base, face up. The ribbon should dangle between the top and the second circles of the base. Bring the two ends of the ribbon up, making sure they've gone under the top circle of the base, and tie a bowtie in front of the cookie neck. Gently lift the legs of the cookie and apply generous dabs of hot glue on the base under the legs and the head. Firmly press the cookie down and hold in place until the glue dries.

5. Continue attaching the cookies until all are used. Tie the wired ribbon on the base with a simple knot and bow.

one 14-inch-diameter wire box frame

1 recipe gingerbread cookies to yield at least fourteen 3 x 2-inch gingerbread boys

gold spray paint (fast-drying kind)

13 yards ⅛-inch wide ribbon

hot glue gun and clear glue sticks

1 yard 2-inch wide wired ribbon

double-sided fir wreath

Gather armfuls of fir to make a double-sided wreath that's as beautiful from the back as it is from the front. To appreciate its two-faced beauty, suspend it on a glass door, from a window, or sling it over the back of a chair or around a fence post.

1. Make a very strong, extra-long hanger between the front and back of the base by knotting the end of one paddle of floral wire to the top middle ring on the back of the base. Unwind about 30 inches of wire, then wrap the paddle around the same middle ring about 5 inches from the first knot. Weave the paddle back and forth between the two spots at least 10 times, each time wrapping it under and over the ring for extra strength. Before cutting the wire, take a 34-inch length and tightly coil it around the length of the loops, then knot securely to the base. Wrap a piece of colored ribbon around the hanger so you can locate it later.

2. Prepare clusters of fir by taking 3 or 4 sprigs and tightly wrapping the bottom 4 inches of the stems with wire from the first paddle. Continue doing this until you have about 100 uniform clusters.

3. Attach the second paddle of wire to the outer ring on the frame. Lay a cluster on the frame. Wrap the wire tightly around 4 inches of the stems several times, then around the wreath frame several times. Do not cut the wire. Turn the frame over and wire on another cluster in the same way, right behind the first. Take a third cluster and place it on the frame about 4 to 5 inches down from the top of the previous one. Again, tightly wrap the paddle of wire around the stems, then around the frame. Turn the wreath over and continue adding clusters of fir in the same way, two by two on each side, always placing them in the same direction and wrapping the wire tightly. To attach the last cluster to each side, gently lift up the needles of the first cluster and wire the last stems under them and around the frame. Cut the wire.

one 18-inch-diameter wire box frame

two 25-foot paddles #22-gauge green floral wire

3 bushels fir sprigs cut 8 to 10 inches long

cameo gift wreath

At holiday times and for special occasions, everyone stretches to come up with beautiful ways to wrap presents. Here is a solution that is not only easy to create but also makes a memorable presentation. It becomes a way to display a gorgeous piece of jewelry that might otherwise remain in a jewelry box, rarely seen. This wreath, with its rare gray cameo, was a Christmas gift and now adorns a dressing table.

one 6-inch-diameter Styrofoam base

3 yards 1½-inch wide wired ribbon

1 straight dressmaker's pin

1 piece of jewelry

1. This wreath will hang by the top knot created in making the wreath, so it needs no special hanger. If you wish to add a separate hanger, make a small one from a 6-inch piece of green floral wire. Slip the wire under a loop in the top knot, shape it into a circle, then twist the ends together.

2. Before beginning, iron out any wrinkles or creases on the ribbon with an iron set on "cool." At the back of the base top, anchor the ribbon to the base with the dressmaker's pin at a point 12 inches in from one end of the ribbon. This excess ribbon will make the knot. Wrap the rest of the ribbon around the base, keeping the spacing even. Where the two ends meet at the top of the base, tie both ends together in a knot. Remove the pin. You want a full look for this simple knot, so don't pull too tightly. The Styrofoam base and ribbon barely weigh anything, so this is not a heavy wreath to support.

3. Pin on the piece of jewelry, and cut the ribbon ends.

ribbon

When working with ribbons or bows, make them look finished by cutting the ends nicely. Cut an inverted triangle, or cut on the diagonal with a sharp point. If you're working with wired ribbon, shape the ribbon ends however you want.

pinecone wreath

For the wreath-maker, long walks through the woods yield not only a sense of well-being but also treasures. Take care that you do not pick any flowers or botanicals in the woods, and check that it is permissible to remove fallen pinecones from the property. Here, the classic pinecone wreath is dressed up in a shimmering metallic cladding as glamorous as a gold lamé evening gown. With the ever-efficient glue gun, it's as simple to make two of these as it is one. The twins would be perfect on a pair of double doors, outside or in.

1. Gather pinecones of similar sizes and shapes. If moist, spread them out on newspaper to dry completely. Spray with several light coatings of paint, allowing them to dry between sprayings. For the most luxurious look, coat the pinecones thoroughly. I sprayed about ¾ of them with antique gold spray, the rest with copper.

2. Decide which side is the back of the wreath; the flatter side should be the front. Make a hanger for the base by cutting at least six 12-inch lengths of floral wire and twisting them together into one strong wire. Attach the wire piece on the top of the outside rim by threading it through several sturdy grapevine branches and twisting the two ends together. Tie a small piece of bright ribbon onto the loop as a marker.

3. Lay the base on a flat surface and position the pinecones around the circle close to one another. At the top, leave a 2½-inch space for the green sash. With the hot glue gun, glue on the two pinecones that flank the sash at the top. Be generous with the glue, but avoid drips. When the glue is set, remove all the other pinecones and hang the wreath up at display height. Now glue on the remaining pinecones

one 20-inch-diameter grapevine base with a flat surface

24 to 36 pinecones of uniform size and shape

1 can antique gold spray paint

1 can copper spray paint

1 paddle #22-gauge green floral wire

hot glue gun and 4 or 5 clear glue sticks

1 yard emerald-green satin or taffeta (at least 38 inches wide), or 1½ yards 3-inch wide ribbon

until the wreath is completed. If you want to work with the wreath on a flat surface, be sure that you don't leave any unsightly glue drips.

4. The sash can be created from fabric or store-bought ribbon. If using 3-inch wide store-bought ribbon, cut the ends on the diagonal for a pretty finish. To make the sash from scratch, cut the fabric into three strips, each 9 x 18 inches. Attach the three pieces by pinning them, right sides together, at the short ends to make one long strip. Machine sew a seam with a 1-inch allowance. Remove the pins and press open. This is now the wrong side of the fabric. Lay the wrong side face down on a flat surface and fold over lengthwise. Pin along the length. Machine stitch a $\frac{1}{2}$-inch seam allowance down the length, leaving a 6-inch gap in the middle for turning right side out. To make the points at the end of the sash, at each end machine stitch a 6-inch diagonal line running from the bottom outer edge to the seam line. Remove the pins and cut away the excess fabric. Position the lengthwise seam in the middle of the sash and press open. Turn right side out and press lightly, placing a damp cloth between the fabric and the iron to protect the fabric. Hand sew the opening closed with small stitches.

5. Slip the sash around the space left at the top of the wreath. Tie a bow, letting the ends hang down. Remove the wreath marker and display in a prominent place.

jingle bell wreath

The humble jingle bell rises to new heights of glory in a wreath that's as spectacular as the holiday season itself. There is glamour in numbers—when massed together by the hundreds, these playful little bells set off sparks on a keepsake wreath you'll love for years and years to come. Jingle bells are available in various sizes in craft shops. Here a hefty ³/₄-inch size is paired with a slightly smaller version in both silver and gold. The bells are sewn onto a base covered in midnight blue velvet for a look that's as bright as the stars in the winter sky.

1. Because the finished wreath is so heavy, you need the extra support that a sewn-on fabric-covered base provides. For the body, fold the velvet in half lengthwise, wrong side out, and pin. Using dressmakers' chalk (or a light-colored drawing pencil) trace a circle with an 18-inch diameter just below the fold line and cut. This will allow enough leftover fabric to cut four strips, each 7 x 27 inches, to make the sash.

2. Center the straw base on one velvet circle and trace the inside ring plus 1¹/₂ inches. Cut out the inner circle; repeat with the second velvet circle. Take one velvet ring and with the right side facing out, pin the outer edge of the fabric to the base. Space the pins closely, about ¹/₄ to ¹/₂ inch apart. Take the other velvet ring, also right side out, and pin it on the other side, overlapping the first. Notch the fabric on the inner rings so the velvet lays flat, covering the inner base. Cut away excess fabric. Secure with pins. Hand sew the velvet on the seams with small stitches. Don't worry if any stitching shows—the base will be covered.

3. To attach the jingle bells, thread the needle with long pieces of the embroidery floss (don't separate the threads.) Then sew on bells one

one 16-inch-diameter straw wreath base (do not remove clear plastic wrap)

1 yard velvet at least 45 inches wide

20 packages ³/₄-inch jingle bells (30 per package)

20 packages ⁵/₈-inch bells (40 per package)

at least 72 straight dressmaker's pins

10 skeins of embroidery floss to match velvet

1 heavyweight needle with large eye

dressmaker's chalk or light-colored pencil

36 inches #22-gauge green floral wire

or two at a time without knotting in between. Add bells until the wreath is covered, leaving a 3-inch space for the sash at the top.

4. To make the sash, pin together the four strips of fabric at the short ends with the right sides facing. Machine stitch a 1-inch seam allowance. You should have a strip measuring 7 x 105 inches. Remove the pins and press the seams open. Fold in half lengthwise with the wrong side out and pin. Machine stitch a seam with a $1/2$-inch allowance down the length, leaving a 6-inch gap in the middle for turning. To make the points at the end of the sash, machine stitch an 8-inch diagonal line running from the bottom outer edge to the seam line. Remove the pins and cut away the excess fabric. Press the lengthwise seams open. Turn right side out and press lightly, placing a damp cloth between the fabric and the iron to protect the velvet. Hand sew the opening closed with small stitches.

5. To make a hanger for the wreath, wrap the floral wire into a 2-inch circle ten times, then coil extra wire around the circle. Slip this over the sash and lay the sash in the space allowed at the top of the base. Position the hanger at the back of the sash, tie the sash into a bow, then sew the hanger onto the sash with several strong stitches. Where the sash meets the velvet base in the back, sew the sash on as well for extra support.

ivy topiary wreath

For centuries, ivy has been a beloved part of the Christmas tradition. Most often associated with holly, ivy was considered to be the feminine counterpart to the prickly evergreen and the two, when combined, were believed to promise fertility to a household. In Victorian times, wreaths of ivy, known as welcome rings were hung at the door. This welcome ring is a topiary version of tenderly tamed ivy designed to be festive year-round. The topiary form is easy to fashion at home, too.

1. Purchase a pot of ivy with leafy, healthy vines that can be trained over the topiary form. If the ivy is in a plastic pot, re-pot it into one of clay.

2. If making a topiary form, use pliers to bend a coat hanger into a circle with a 10-inch diameter, leaving 4 extra inches on each end. Twist the ends together and cover the form with green floral tape.

3. Gently insert the topiary form into the soil. Divide the ivy vines evenly on both sides of the form and, starting with the longest vines, wrap them around the form, alternating sides until all the vines are wrapped. Pinch off any small side shoots and use the raffia to attach any recalcitrant vines. Water well and set on the saucer. Tie the ribbon around the pot with a bow in the front.

4. Place in the sun for a few hours each day. As new shoots appear, train them around the form.

1 circular topiary form with a 10-inch diameter (available at craft stores) or 1 wire coat hanger

one 8-inch-diameter pot of ivy

one 8-inch clay pot and saucer

needle-nosed pliers

1 roll green floral tape

3 or 4 pieces raffia

2½ yards 2-inch wide wired ribbon

boxwood wreath

At Christmastime, the woods offer tremendous possibilities for the wreath-maker. There are boughs of graceful fir, gleaming boxwood, and pungent pine all waiting to be cut and made into decorations for the home. Here, the boughs were wound into a very easy-to-make yet elegant wreath that would enhance any setting. Vary the amount of greens to achieve the fullness you prefer.

1. If making the base, shape the wire or coat hanger into a circle and twist both ends into loops. Hook the loops together, then close them with pliers, flattening the loops as much as possible.

2. Cover the base with green floral tape.

3. To make clusters with the greens, place them in separate piles. Take one piece each of fir, balsam, and boxwood, and tightly wrap the bottom 3 inches of the stems several times with floral wire.

4. Attach the paddle of floral wire to the base. Place a cluster across the base with its stems toward the inside and its top angled outward. Wrap the stems tightly with the wire several times, covering about 5 inches. Do not cut the wire. Add the second cluster about 5 inches down from the top of the previous cluster. Wire onto the base. Continue adding on clusters until the base is covered. Add the last cluster by gently lifting up the top of the first, then wiring on the last. Cut the wire.

one 12-inch-diameter wire ring base made of #16-gauge wire or 1 wire coat hanger

12 boughs of evergreens about 10 inches long: boxwood, fir, balsam

1 roll green floral tape

1 paddle #22-gauge green floral wire

fresh fir

Boughs of evergreen are best used soon after cutting. Crush the woody stems, then stand them in a bucket of water for 12 hours for maximum freshness.

index

Entries and page numbers in bold refer to individual wreath instructions.